Whippets

Whippets

Jane Eastoe

Illustrations by Meredith Jensen

BATSFORD

First published in the United Kingdom in 2022 by

B. T. Batsford Ltd
43 Great Ormond Street
London WC1N 3HZ

An imprint of B. T. Batsford Holdings Limited

Copyright © B.T. Batsford Ltd 2022
Text © Jane Eastoe 2022
Illustrations © Meredith Jensen 2022

ISBN: 9781849947923

A CIP catalogue record for this book
is available from the British Library.

10 9 8 7 6 5 4 3 2 1

Reproduction by Rival Colour Ltd, UK
Printed in Italy by L.E.G.O. SpA

FSC
www.fsc.org
MIX
Paper | Supporting
responsible forestry
FSC® C023419

Contents

Whippets

Introduction

Let me introduce myself: I am a whippet, absolutely the best breed you could choose. The crème de la crème. Other breeds may tell you the same thing, but just take a look at the evidence. I am an athlete, a beautifully proportioned physical specimen. I like to think of myself as the supermodel of the dog world. I am elegant. The greyhound, my close relative, is handsome, certainly, but not as refined as the whippet. The Italian greyhound, who is notably smaller and lighter than me, is also speedy, but does not quite have my beautiful line.

My breed was only formally recognized by the British Kennel Club in 1891, but my type has been popular for centuries. We have featured in paintings and statuary throughout history, and in the grandest houses we have been immortalized for posterity, curled up with our owners on their tombs.

But back to me. I have excellent manners and I am not pushy, greedy or noisy. As dogs go, I am remarkably clean. I don't like mud, I might paddle in the river but rarely much more than that, and I certainly won't arrive back at your side covered in smelly pond weed. Like a cat, I will lick myself clean, although

I do not slobber. My coat is short and fine, so expensive trips to the grooming parlour are not a necessity.

I don't bark very often, so you're highly unlikely to get complaints from the neighbours about the noise. I may bark when someone comes to the front door or if I am excited to see another dog. I am talkative; I will whimper if I am cold, or if I want a favourite toy that has rolled under the sofa, or a dog chew that I know is in the cupboard. I might even yowl with excitement in the car when I think we are getting close to one of my favourite walks.

I don't like to be cold and I hate the rain. If it's pouring, I will nip outside to relieve myself, but I won't appreciate a long walk, certainly not without a good waterproof coat and even then I won't be happy until I can curl up back at home in the dry.

I am very loyal and loving. My idea of heaven is lying beside you on the sofa, preferably with a blanket. If you give me the opportunity I will not only sleep on your bed, but under the duvet with you. Wherever I sleep, I will require a good soft mattress and a blanket I can snuggle under. On the subject of sleep, I am not naturally an early riser and quite enjoy a lie-in. If you are asleep, I will doze contentedly until you get up.

With regard to exercise, many people mistakenly think that whippets need masses of exercise. However, it's important to remember that we are sprinters, not marathon runners. We LOVE to run. We are built to run. Running is our happy place. We show off to other dogs; 'Chase me, chase me,' we might say, before taking off like a speeding bullet. Off-lead running in a safe space is important to us, but after 30 minutes of exercise we are content to curl up quietly. We do appreciate two such walks a day, unless, of course, it's raining, in which case – as I mentioned earlier – we would prefer a very short walk. A wet whippet is a miserable whippet.

On the whole, we are mild-mannered, not known for any aggressive tendencies. We generally like other dogs and aren't inclined to start a fight, which makes for relaxed walks.

Whippets are sighthounds; our breed was developed to hunt but we use our eyes rather than our nose. Given half the chance, we will take off after rabbits, hares, squirrels and deer. At the sight of such prey we tend to become deaf to all calls. We can tolerate other animals at home, such as cats and chickens, if introduced as puppies, but these are *our* cats and *our* chickens. We will not have the same regard for any other cats or wildlife outside the home: we will chase them and we may kill them. Not to put too fine a point on it, you can never trust us off lead with wildlife or farm animals.

Children, on the other hand, we rather like. Curious creatures, they have a variety of toys that are of endless interest, especially anything squeaky. Children also seem to be in possession of a lot of small snacks, which we are more than happy to share or steal. We like being stroked and petted, so enjoy the attentions of children, and we are really quite patient and tolerant, although we do have our limits. At worst we might snap but will usually give some warning growls first if we are getting fed up. If the attention gets too much, we are likely to take ourselves off to find some peace and quiet rather than cause any upset.

Whippets are an intelligent breed, but we are not slavish and can't always see the point of doing what you want us to. We quite enjoy short bursts of training, but as we are not especially food orientated the incentive is not always there. High-status treats like cheese, chicken or ham help to maintain our focus; a standard dog biscuit might motivate a labrador, but it won't do much for us. We are also quite sensitive, so need a gentle, patient teacher.

Recall is probably the single most import piece of our training. Basically, you will never, ever catch us unless we willingly return to you.

Whippets are like heat-seeking missiles: we gravitate to any source of warmth. We like to bask in the sun like cats, so keep an eye on us as we can get sunburnt if we are allowed to stay out for too long. For this same reason, we appreciate being wrapped up in a fleece or a jumper when the weather is cold. This is not an affectation: whippets are naturally lean, and with no fat and short fur coats we struggle to maintain our body temperature and will shiver uncontrollably. Some whippets are more robust and manage the cold better than others, but take your cue from us – we will probably need wrapping up in cold weather.

Our deep chests will require you buy garments designed specifically for us, otherwise they will rub when we run. If we start running around a lot, you may need to remove our coats so that we don't overheat. This is not as much trouble as it seems, and we will obligingly lift up our paws for you once we get used to being dressed.

How will we reward you for all this effort? We are incredibly loyal and form a deep attachment to our owners and their wider family. Ideally, we like to be close to you. You are our whole world, aside from rabbits. We won't be a bother: give us a bed and we will curl up, preferably in the same room as you, and we will stay there until we sense the next walk is coming up.

Didn't I say we were the best breed you could choose?

Bowie

Owned by Peter | Lives in Ontario, Canada | @whippetbowie

Bowie loves chasing squirrels, playing with
frisbees, and eating (in no particular order). He's
super smart: his most impressive trick is jumping
into people's arms on command.

Puppies

As a puppy I don't look much like my adult form. I am not long of limb or muscular, my snout is of regular proportion, but right from the start I have those melting whippet eyes. These will be dark blue to begin with, but gradually mature to brown.

My idea of heaven is either to snuggle up with my siblings in a great, warm pile of puppies or to tear around like a mad thing, tripping over my feet. Our breeders will assess us all with a critical eye, analyzing which they think are the finest physical specimens with the potential for a future in the show ring.

When you come to meet us for the first time you will be questioned carefully by the breeder about what you want from us. Do you want a show dog, a breeding dog or a pet? What kind of a pet do you want: loving or lively? Depending on your answers, you may only be shown a couple of puppies to choose from that best suit your requirements.

You should meet my mother and quite possibly some of my other relatives too. My father might not be around to view as he may live some distance away, but you should see a picture of him at the least.

A litter of whippet puppies is adorable but let me give you some words of wisdom: even if you plan to have two dogs, don't get them from the same litter at the same time. Whippets have selective hearing at the best of times, but if you take me and one of my siblings, we will become very reliant on one another and will pay you little heed. What's more, as we mature, we may fight to determine which is the dominant whippet in the pack. If you want two whippets (and why wouldn't you?), start with one and only get a second when the first is well trained. The first dog will lead the way with all the basic training techniques.

Preparing My Home

Once a sale has been agreed, you should make a few preparations at home.

- **Security** Please check that your garden has adequate fencing – I am a great escapologist and when small I can, and will, wriggle through very small holes or gaps in the fencing. Repair as required or plug small holes with logs or chicken wire. Once I grow this will become less of an issue, but as my limbs lengthen, so my ability to leap over things will increase.

- **Bed** I will need a lovely soft bed, but you'll probably find that a big adult one may overwhelm me. Initially, it is good to have something with nice soft sides so that I am protected from draughts. This will also stop me slipping off in my sleep, as I am quite lightweight to begin with and tend to just slide off big flat beds and end up on the floor. Soft cloth baskets with tall sides and a cushion inside will suit me very well when I am little. I get quite attached to my bed and as I grow you may find me determinedly wedged into my tiny puppy bed just to prove that I still fit. Whippets can fold up very small!

- **Crate** You might want to get me a crate, not to keep me in, but to give me a nice safe bolthole. I will appreciate it if you cover this over with a blanket so it stays nice and warm, and a heated pad will simulate the warmth of my siblings. If you put paper or a puppy pad on the floor of the crate I can relieve myself in the night. I never usually soil my bed, but accidents happen, and when I am very small, I will need to pee during the night.

- **Bowls** Buy two bowls, one for food and one for water, which you'll leave down for me the whole time. Stainless steel is durable and easy to keep clean.

- **Poo bags** You should also purchase a supply of poo bags so you can dispose of my poo; compostable bags are available.

- **Toys** Please buy me some toys. I will want to chew and I am very playful. If I start to nibble your fingers you can give me a toy to chew on instead – my teeth are like needles! I will get the message that

one is acceptable and the other is not. Balls, soft toys (I love anything that squeaks but will remove all the stuffing with terrifying speed and the squeaker must be taken away from me as it can be dangerous). Squeaky toys should only be allowed under supervision. I will still love the empty fluffy part of the toy so don't throw that away! Harder toys are helpful for teething.

- **Collar and lead** You may also want to get me a lightweight puppy collar and a lead, even though you won't actually be able to take me

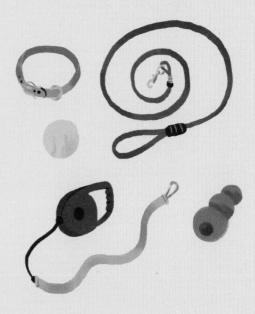

out for a walk for a few weeks. Until my vaccinations kick in, it's simply not safe for me to mix with other dogs, or to be anywhere that other dogs have been. Always make sure you can slip two fingers underneath the collar when it is around my neck and remember to check regularly, I will grow quickly and tight collars are uncomfortable. If you put a collar around my neck early, and put me on the lead to play, I will get used to it before you take me out on my first walk.

House Rules

It is a good idea to agree house rules in advance of my arrival. Am I going to have the run of the house, be limited to the downstairs or only be allowed in certain rooms under supervision? Am I going to be allowed on the sofa or the beds? Am I going to be given treats from the table? I need consistency and clarity and will challenge boundaries.

Please scour the house in advance for things that I might chew or eat that could be harmful. I am like a toddler and cannot be trusted to be sensible.

Things to Hide Out of Sight

- Your shoes
- Electric wires, plugs and cables
- Your shoes
- Children's toys
- Your shoes
- Medicine or chocolate in your handbag or briefcase, or lying around
- Your shoes
- Slug pellets, mouse traps and garden chemicals
- Your shoes
- Painkillers
- Your shoes
- Cleaning products – plastic bottles are very tempting to chew
- Your underwear – not as hazardous but potentially highly embarrassing should I appear in front of your guests with a pair of pants in my mouth.

Training Basics

Training starts from day one, but before you leap to Chapter 2 make sure that everyone in your household grasps the basic principles. Agree together in advance what specific training words you will use; I will understand clear one-word instructions much faster. Use 'Sit' – not 'Sit down' (though whippets don't much like sitting); if you want me to lie down on the floor say 'Down' – not 'Lie down'; 'Wait' if you want me to stay in one place until summoned; 'Stay' – if you want me to remain where I am until *you* return to me. I will also need a trigger word for going to the toilet, see below.

House training

Please familiarize yourself with the principles of house training a whippet in advance. Start collecting newspapers or buy puppy pads in preparation. It is much harder to house train us when the weather is cold than when it's warm, and you can leave the doors open all the time. If you get a whippet puppy in the winter do buy them a coat (even though they will grow out if it very quickly). I promise you it's worth it for toilet training alone. As I said before, a cold whippet is a miserable whippet. Instead of sniffing around to find somewhere to wee I will simply shiver piteously and huddle by the back door.

Don't leave me in the garden alone. I like to be with you so will only worry about where you've gone and not focus on weeing or pooing. Put on your coat and stay out with me. That way you can give me lots of praise when I do the deed.

While I am a puppy, I will probably want to pee every time I wake up from a sleep and also to pee and or poo straight after every meal, so take me outside as much as you can. Every time I use the outdoor facilities, I am making scents that will trigger a similar response next time. As a general rule, I need to be taken outside every two hours – hourly is even better. Try to stay outside with me for a bit after I have done my business, play with me and let us have some fun – you are rewarding me for being good.

Agree on a key word you will use for toilet training – make this a word you don't use frequently in general

conversation – my owner uses 'Bumbles'! Use the agreed word when I am peeing or pooing: say it over and over again quietly and gently. Don't tell me that I am a 'Good girl' or a 'Good boy' as this may become my trigger word to urinate.

I will quickly learn that when you use this trigger word you want me to wee or poo, such as last thing at night or before you are about to leave me in the house when you are going out. If everyone does this, I will learn what you want me to do much faster. Make a HUGE fuss of me every time I pee or poo outside, I need to understand that you are happy when I do this!

Make a note of where I like to pee outside and take me to that area when you want me to use the facilities. Some dogs like a dry surface, such as gravel, stone or concrete, some will only wee on grass – we all have our preferences.

At night I can last for about four to five hours without weeing. Some owners set an alarm to take their puppy out; others keep one ear open and whisk us outside if they hear us wriggling. It all depends on where I am sleeping.

If I do have an accident don't shout at me. Say 'NO!' loudly if you catch me in the act and carry me into the garden, then praise me effusively when I wee. I am a sensitive soul and shouting will only frighten me and make me nervous. It might also make me hide away when I need to wee, which will just compound the problem. Gentle handling is required and lots of praise and rewards when I get things right. Whippets are smart. I will catch on quickly. Clean up the accident area with an enzymatic cleaning material; biological washing powder mixed with warm water in a 1:9 ratio will remove all hint of a smell. If you don't do this, I will always be tempted to return to the same spot. Household disinfectants should be avoided as they contain ammonia and the smell of this may encourage me to soil the same area again.

The Journey Home

We puppies usually leave our families from the age of eight weeks old, by which time I will be weaned, but be prepared, I will come with a list of dietary requirements for the first few months and my breeder should give you some of the kibble I have been eating to help me settle in with you. This should help avoid tummy upsets. I will have been microchipped, wormed and may have had my first inoculation. You will also be given my Kennel Club documents, which have full details of my lineage.

The journey to my new home may be trying. Remember, I have probably never been in a car, and I may cry for my siblings. I may be car sick, I might pee or even poo. On the other hand, I might just fall asleep on your lap and stay that way for the whole journey. It is a good idea to have some old towels and some kitchen roll to hand so you can easily deal with all eventualities. You might even want to pack a change of clothes – don't wear anything precious! If I am car sick, I will grow out of it. Long term, whippets tend to be good travellers – we enjoy a car journey and survey the landscape with interest or peer over your shoulder like the worst back-seat driver. We find long motorway journeys boring and tend to sleep until the car comes to a halt.

If I am car sick as a puppy, don't let me develop a phobia about the car. Keep putting me in it for a few minutes. Stay with me and give me treats. We don't need to go anywhere. Then take me round the block a few times on a short journey so I learn that being in the car is not a scary experience.

When we arrive home for the first time, put me down in the garden to give me a chance to relieve pent-up tensions! Stay with me.

Welcome to Your New Home

When you bring me into the house, put me down and let me sniff around for a little while. Please don't overwhelm me with attention, especially if there are children in the house. Let me go to them and sniff them. Let me take things at my own pace. This will be a frightening experience. Show me my bed and some toys. Show me where my water bowl can be found. When I have had a little time, give me something to eat, then take me outside straight away and give me the chance to do my business.

The First Night (Start as You Mean to Go on)

Given the choice, I will sleep with you, in your bed. I know, I know, dog trainers do not advocate this technique but there's not a whippet owner alive who won't admit that their dogs all aim for this nirvana. We are quite a quietly determined breed, and we will be sad and lonely without our siblings and without you. We will cry, we may wail, and we may even emit an eerie howl. If you can't cope with this, keep me close for a few nights until I have settled in. Some people tuck the puppy bed beside theirs, some people put the puppy bed up near their pillows so they can stroke us, then put it on the floor after a few nights. Other people might bring me into bed with them. Then, when I wake up and start wriggling, you will know that I need to wee and you can take me out. I will be very happy with this arrangement.

If you do weaken, please be warned, I will spend the rest of my life trying to crawl into bed with you. The only way of breaking this habit will be to shut me in a crate at night. You can soften the blow by placing the crate in your bedroom. Knowing you are close at hand will give me some comfort, and I will get used to sleeping by myself in time.

If you really want to pamper me, you can purchase beds that have a top cover as well as a soft mattress – I burrow my way in nose first and settle down happily. This will not be your cheapest option, but it saves having to fiddle around with doggy blankets or duvets. Yes, I do love a duvet and if I can't be under yours, my own is the next best option. I will cry in the night if I get cold.

In my house we are not allowed either on or in the bed, and that is a hard and fast rule. However, when our pack leader goes away, we whippets jump into bed with the second-in-command and snuggle up. Utter bliss!

Healthy Eating

After the first night with me, it will be time to tackle my dietary requirements. Whippet puppies have four to five small meals a day. My breeder should give you a sample menu and some of the packet food I

Olive

Owned by Catherine | Lives in London | @the.london.whippet

Olive is a beach lover but hates the water, is
super fast but extremely clumsy. She truly lives
up to the whippet reputation of being a 'velcro
dog'; she is happiest when curled up next to you.

have been eating to avoid any tummy upsets from dietary changes.

My gourmet puppy menu plan may startle you, but I will not always need to eat this way. As puppies we often have porridge for breakfast, scrambled eggs mid-morning, some kibble early afternoon, a little dog meat in the early evening and perhaps a small snack last thing at night. I also enjoy some puppy milk. Whippets are not naturally greedy dogs, so I may eat something happily one day and turn my nose up at it the next. Don't leave my food down for longer than ten minutes at a time, even if I eat nothing, and don't offer me food until my next mealtime.

As a small puppy, I will need four meals a day, nicely spaced out please. At 12 weeks I can drop to three meals a day, and at six months I will be ready for just two meals a day.

Recall

Start working on this as soon as you have settled on my name. Have treats to hand. Call my name in a slightly higher pitched voice than usual and sound excited. When I come to you reward me with a treat and make a HUGE fuss of me. Let me go then repeat. If I don't come to you try running away from me and call me; reward me when I come. Make it a fun game. Stick to my name only – no other words, not 'Here', not 'Come', just my name.

Treats

Keep treats strictly for training purposes – don't give me anything off your plate, as much as I gaze at you with big, hopeful eyes. This will be hard because as I grow, I will become an expert in emotional blackmail. Try to remain resolute. If you feed me once from your plate, I will thereafter expect a taste of everything, and be warned, if the opportunity presents itself, I will not hesitate to help myself if you are not around. Nothing edible is safe. I am a natural thief.

The Vet

Most vets like you to register with them as soon as you get a puppy. They will give me a once-over to check I am doing okay, weigh me, test my microchip, get my vaccination schedules in place and discuss flea and tick treatments. They will also make a fuss of me so that my first visit to the vet is a positive experience. Vets will probably know about puppy socialization classes in the area and usually have lists of useful contacts for the future, such as kennels and dog sitters.

The vaccination schedule varies slightly from country to country, so be guided by your vet. Some diseases require me to have an annual booster to ensure continued protection. The vet will advise you and will normally send out a reminder. All these diseases are extremely unpleasant and are easily passed on. Please make sure I am vaccinated as a puppy and that you maintain my annual booster-jab schedule to keep me safe.

Keep your vaccination certificates safe. The vet can update them as required and you will have to show them if you need to put me into kennels. No reputable kennels can take an unvaccinated dog.

A rabies vaccination is required in some countries and will be needed if you intend to travel internationally with me. This is not a quick process; rabies vaccinations need time to become effective and I have to have blood tests to ensure I have sufficient immunity. Allow an absolute minimum of six to eight months for this process. You will also need to ensure that I have annual rabies boosters.

Vaccinations

The following vaccinations are required in most countries:

- Canine distemper
- Hepatitis
- Leptospirosis
- Parvovirus

Collar and Lead

While I am in quarantine and have to be carried about in the big wide world, take the opportunity to get me used to both my collar and lead. Be forewarned, I will not enjoy this experience. Start with the collar: put it on for a few

minutes, give me treats, then take it off. Once I have had a few days to get used to the collar, try me with the lead – just a few minutes at a time for both. Lots of treats please.

Social Niceties

All dogs benefit from puppy socialization as soon as their vaccination schedule permits. We whippets tend to be quite friendly, but are a naturally cautious breed, especially when we are on the lead and can't run for our lives if needs be. Submissive weeing is quite common when we are little – it's just our way of showing that we know our place – so outside socializing might be a good idea. Some of us can be quite nervous, so we need socialization classes even more.

Be gentle with us – you might need to just sit and watch the class with us until we stop tail tucking and look sufficiently interested in the proceedings.

When puppies mingle, expect a lot of bottom sniffing. For some reason, you humans seem to find this ritual impolite, but it is simply our way of saying hello. Try not to mind. Please don't tell us off for doing what comes naturally. It also teaches us to recognize the signals that another dog might not be so friendly – if a strange dog stands with a stiff body and tail, with its hackles rising and ears back, I have to learn to back off.

Puppy socialization classes usually include some element of group training and help to teach you how to get me to focus on you even when there are

serious distractions around. They also teach you dog-training techniques. Let's be frank about this, these classes are as much for you as they are for me. You have to learn how to handle me effectively so I will behave beautifully for you. You might think I'll never learn how to do anything, but the dog trainer will show you, with terrifying ease, how easy it is to get me to do what you want.

Don't blame me if I behave badly – basically it's all down to you. Keep on with my training every day and just wait to see how smart I am. Remember, there are no bad dogs, just bad owners.

Remember also to take poo bags with you and treats – lots of them – it will help you to keep me focused on you and what you want me to do.

Nervous Puppies

Some whippet puppies are quite bold and bumptious, but others suffer from anxiety. They need kind and gentle handling. Pheromone collars that mimic the smell of mum can be helpful. A shivering whippet may be cold or excited – don't automatically assume we are shivering with fear. Tail-tucking is a better indicator: when we tuck our tails firmly between our legs and right up underneath our bodies, we are signalling that we are uneasy.

Try not to reinforce nervous behaviour. If your puppy hates being away from you, encourage them to play then leave the room for a moment. Keep playing and popping back so they get more confident that you will return.

The same applies to teaching me to get used to being home alone. Only leave me alone for a few minutes initially so I don't get the chance to panic. Tire me out before you leave so that hopefully I'll just fall asleep. Build up the time you leave me little by little, starting with just five minutes.

If I am nervous of other dogs, don't scoop me up out of harm's way. This will only reinforce the idea that I am in grave danger. Talk to other dog owners and ask if it is okay to stroke their pets and talk to them, but don't push me forwards. Let me see you being open and friendly and let me build my confidence at my own pace.

Travelling Companions

If you take your whippet puppy on trains, buses and the underground when they are small they may be fearful at first, but they will get used to it and behave calmly. Car travel, though you might not think it, has more restrictions.

In the UK, the Highway Code states that dogs and other animals must be suitably restrained. The interpretation of this is quite loose, but for your sake and mine, please ensure that proper restraints are in place. Quite apart from the fact that you adore me and don't want any harm to come to me if we have an accident, please remember that if I come hurtling through the car at speed I can injure you in precisely the same way another human can if they are unrestrained in the rear of the car.

The most effective way to keep me safe is to have a crate in the rear of your car to minimise the distance I can be flung in a crash. If you accustom me to the crate at home I will be perfectly content to travel in this. Dog harnesses that clip on to seat belts can be utilised if a crate is not an option. These should not be used in the front seat as if an air bag goes off in an accident it could seriously harm your dog. Dog guards that stop me from clambering into the front of the car can be fitted, but ideally these should be used in conjunction with a crate.

Hormones and Bitches

As I move towards my first birthday and the end of puppyhood, the hormones start to kick in; in developmental

terms a one-year-old whippet is the equivalent of a 15-year-old human. Most female whippets will have their first season (pro-oestrus) between the ages of one or two, but some can go into heat earlier than this. Vets advise that female whippets should have one season before they are spayed, so brace yourselves that you are going to have to cope with at least one season.

Whippet bitches tend to come into heat every 11–13 months. However, the frequency of seasons can vary depending on when her first season begins. Some whippets can have two seasons a year. Very young bitches who come into heat should not be allowed to breed; it can be dangerous for them to have puppies before they are fully grown.

Your bitch will be on heat for around 21 days, and she may well become cranky. And for good reason: her vulva will swell, as may her nipples, and she will bleed; she will also need to urinate more frequently. Whippets are acutely conscious of the fact that they are bleeding. They keep themselves very clean. Nevertheless they will drop blood – not excessively, but there will be spots here and there. There are a number of ways of dealing with this, but please bear in mind that as well as being cranky, your whippet bitch will also be clingy and want to be with you. Isolating her in a room with hard flooring will make her miserable if she is used to being with you.

Nowadays you can buy pants for bitches on heat. She can wear these in the house, but she may take great exception to this addition to her wardrobe – remember, it will stop her from keeping herself clean. You can cover her bedding and the sofa with towels and wash them regularly, and you can cover carpeted areas of the floor with towels or newspaper. You can spot clean spots as they appear and then have your carpet professionally cleaned when she has finished her season. Try not to let any irritation show – she will pick up on this.

Keep her in close contact when she is on heat. Male dogs will find her irresistible and they can pick up her pheromone-filled scent from a long way away. Only let her off lead when you can do so safely or choose to walk her at times of the day when there will be fewer dogs around to bother her. If she has her first season young, she may not be desperate to mate, but whippets are escape artists, and if your garden isn't very secure don't take any risks with her welfare, as you don't want a litter of unwanted puppies.

If you also have a complete male dog in the house, your life is about to get very difficult. One option is to persuade a friend to look after your male dog until your bitch has finished her season; alternatively, keep your dogs separate. The use of stair gates or crates allows the two dogs to still see each other, but not to interact.

Neutering your whippet bitch once she has had her first season will give

her protection against some forms of cancer and pyometra (infection of the uterus). She does not need a litter of puppies to be happy.

Some bitches can get very uncomfortable when they are on heat and a trip to the vet may be required. The vulva may become painfully swollen and constant cleaning can aggravate this problem. If her nipples become distended, she may be producing milk and will require medication to stop production.

Once your whippet bitch has had her first season, speak to the vet about having her neutered. This is a straightforward operation and dogs recover very quickly. There is a cost involved, but a litter of unwanted puppies is far, far more expensive in terms of cost. Leave breeding pedigree puppies to the professionals. If you plan to breed from your bitch, make sure you seek professional advice from a breeder – there is a lot to learn, aside from the complex business of birthing.

Hormones and Male Dogs

Most male whippets are fertile when they are fully mature, somewhere between 12 and 15 months. However, some dogs can be capable of siring puppies much earlier – you have been warned.

Just like teenage boys, we may sometimes act before we think – the testosterone is surging! Indeed, for a short while young male dogs have more testosterone than adult dogs, and this can lead to a sudden outbreak of territorial behaviour. Scent marking territory is an early indication of sexual maturity. Your male whippet will continually stop for short wees to signal where he has been. You may also find to your horror that a perfectly house-trained whippet suddenly lets you down by peeing inside a friend's house, or in a shop or pub. This can happen with all breeds, not just whippets. Please always own up to my offence and offer to clean up the puddle.

Perfectly amiable whippets can suddenly start having stand-offs with other dogs. Don't panic, this doesn't necessarily mean your sweet boy is going to become an aggressive monster. Male dogs have to deal with a whole new set of signals from other males, who may suddenly be aggressive with them. Your puppy needs to learn to re-evaluate the social signals he is getting. He will learn. Whippets tend not to be aggressive dogs, and if they get into a fight, they tend to come off worse with their thin skins and short coats.

If you are having to deal with some aggression for the first time, try not to panic. You will need to exercise your dog well and increase training; reinforcing good behaviour will help. If you are struggling, seek help from a professional dog trainer, who will have strategies that will help you and your whippet to cope.

A large number of dogs that are given up for rescue are adolescents. As for humans, this can be a challenging time for behaviour; help your puppy transition smoothly to adulthood with kindness, plenty of exercise and lots of positive training. We will reward you in the long term.

Training

If I come to you as a puppy, it may be a month or more before you can start taking me out and about on regular walks, and that is when our day-to-day life begins. At first, everyone will coo over me because I am adorable. As I grow, we will both be judged on how we behave, and not just on my good looks.

You must be top dog – the 'pack leader' whose rules I follow. If you don't assume this position by teaching me to do what you say, I will try to assume the pack-leader position. Please believe me when I say that I am a terrible decision-maker – left to my own devices I'd think nothing of chasing a rabbit onto a four-lane motorway. You must assume the pack-leader role to keep us both safe.

Dog Training

Attending puppy socialization classes and dog-training lessons will help us both to develop a good relationship, and will help you to teach me good manners and how to behave. Please remember that I do not speak your language; you will have to patiently teach me how to do what you want. I won't understand the words, but I will learn what you want me to do when you make certain sounds.

The Basic Rules of Dog Training

- You must have a lead with you every time we go out and use it when necessary to keep me safe on the roads, when signage requests it or around livestock. Never let me roam unsupervised.
- Don't let me approach cyclists, runners or other dog owners unless invited. Always put me on the lead if you see a horse and rider.
- Don't let me race off lead across private land or through crops – whippets love to run through wheat fields looking for rabbits; keep us under control so we can't be tempted.
- Never let me worry or chase livestock.
- Be safe around livestock. Check fields before entering so you are not caught unawares. Maintain a good distance from livestock and give them plenty of space. Cattle and horses can be quite curious about dogs, and very protective if they have calves or foals. If livestock comes worryingly close, release me so that I can get away and you can too.
- Always bag up my poo and carry it with you. This can be disposed of in special dog-poo bins or, if none are around, in any public litter bin.
- Don't leave bags of poo on the path to pick up later or hang them from tree branches. Pick up as you go.
- Put an identification tag on my collar with your contact details on it. Put *your* name on it and a phone number. Remember to update this and my microchip details if we move house.
- Keep my vaccination and worming treatments up to date.

Learning appropriate hand signals will help me to further understand what you want. Training dogs is not difficult, but it requires time and patience from you. Two short, five-minute sessions daily will help me learn. If you put in the effort I will repay you, most of the time anyway, by behaving beautifully.

Recall

This is the most important lesson that I will learn, given that I can move so much faster than you. Some of us learn to come to our names quickly and easily, some are rather more wilful. Even when you think we have mastered this technique, I can guarantee we will let you down spectacularly when it suits us, and as teenagers (around 10–11 months old) we can become quite stroppy and uncooperative and develop selective hearing, just like you humans.

If this happens, just reinforce your original technique with lots of repetition. Call me back repeatedly and reward me with high-status treats. Whippets don't sit very comfortably so you might not want to make me sit to get a treat. Instead, hold the treat in a clenched fist and make me touch your hand with my nose, then release the treat. Use the words 'Off you go' to tell me I can go away and play again. Repeat and repeat at random times throughout the walk.

If you only do this at the end of the walk, I will learn that it is not a good idea to come back to you. It is best to get me on the lead before the end of the walk when I just think I am returning for another treat. Try to keep one step ahead of me mentally, if not physically.

Lavish praise upon me every time I come back to you. Then lavish some more praise. As I become more reliable, you will notice that I keep looking back to check where you are. This is a good sign – it indicates that I am attuned to you, that you are important to me and that I want to keep an eye on you, so you don't suddenly disappear.

A whistle can be a very useful tool. It will save you from having to bellow my name as I vanish into the distant horizon at 30 miles an hour. Plus, a whistle expresses no emotion, so I won't pick up on any

Orla & Beau

Owned by Donna | Live in Lancashire, England | @whippetfamily

Beau is a courageous bone-cancer survivor,
having beaten all the odds against her. Orla is
her fun-loving partner in crime. They are loyal,
obedient, quick, and super clever.

anger in your voice if you are getting frustrated.

If am not behaving and run you ragged trying to catch me, don't ever shout at me when I finally come within grasp. This will only make me apprehensive of returning to you – I won't understand why sometimes you give me a treat and sometimes you shout.

If I am proving to be very resistant to recall, try not feeding me before a walk and keep those high-status treats to hand on the walk. If all else fails, I will do almost anything for cheese.

If I am still not responsive to recall, you can try hand-feeding my meals in the garden for about a fortnight. Your hands will get very messy, but I will follow you around devotedly as you feed me a little bit at a time. This helps to reinforce the message that you are the source of all good things and coming to you brings real benefits.

Long trainer leads are also an option. These are designed to drag along behind me as I run free but give you a better chance of catching me when you call. These are best used when you are able to stamp your foot on my lead.

Call or whistle me in; if I don't respond immediately, pull me gently back in, reward me and release me. A trainer lead has the potential to be a minor health-and-safety issue for you. If I run behind you at high speed, only to race off again, I might pull your feet out from under you. You have been warned.

Basic Commands

Keep training sessions short and please don't bother me with training if I have just had a meal or if I am tired – all I will be interested in is sleeping and not learning. Pick the moment when I am likely to be at my most receptive. If I have just woken up and I am doing high-speed circuits of the garden, you might also find it hard to keep me focused.

Sit

Whippets are not natural sitters; it is not a particularly comfortable position for us. Left to our own devices, we prefer to stand or lie down, as long as the ground is comfortable and dry. Please bear this in mind when trying to train me.

Put a treat in your hand in a fist. Hold your hand over my nose and say 'Sit'.

Lift your hand slightly upwards and backwards – as I lift my nose up to follow the treat, I will naturally drop my bottom and go into a sit. Praise me.

Once I have grasped this command, practise saying it with me beside you as well as in front of you.

Get me to sit before you give me my meals.

Down

Start this training once I have begun to grasp the 'Sit' command. For good results, do this training where I can lie down comfortably, either on my bed or on a rug. I am skinny; if you want me to lie down, I need padding on my ribcage.

Get me to 'Sit' and reward me. Put another treat in the palm of your hand, say 'Down'. Then move your hand slowly towards the ground, edging it just out of reach as my nose follows your hand. I will lower my front legs and with a bit of luck my hindquarters will follow. If I get up to try to reach the treat, just pop me back in the sit position, give me a treat, then try 'Down' again. It might take a few attempts before I figure out what you want me to do, but I will get there.

Once I am beginning to grasp this instruction, you might like to introduce a hand signal to support it. With the treat in the palm of your hand, extend your index finger and point it downwards. Take the treat to my nose and repeat the same process with your hand so that I lie down. Make a huge fuss of me every time I get this right.

In time, when I have grasped the basic principle, start practising the command away from my bed.

Wait

The wait command teaches me to stay where I am until you tell me what to do next. I'll stay in the car with this command while you find my lead and get me attached – without knowing this command, I might just leap past you and race off. I'll wait until you put my food bowl on the floor and won't dance on my hind legs trying to reach the bowl you are holding. I'll wait at gates and doors while you go ahead of me.

To teach me 'Wait', first tell me to 'Sit', then take a step backwards, still facing me, holding your palm up. Come back to me and praise me. You'll probably have to do a lot of practice before I start waiting. Just keep up with short bursts of training and I'll get the message. Keep distances very small and gradually extend them as I am following the instruction reliably. It doesn't matter if I lie down instead of sitting, just so long as I stay put. In time, you will be able to leave me sitting and waiting while you walk a distance away and I will remain there until you call me.

Use 'Wait' every time you feed me. Make me sit, then tell me to wait until my food bowl is on the floor. I will keep getting up and trying to rush it, but just raise the bowl, put me back in the sit position and tell me to 'Wait' again. If you do this at each mealtime, it is an easy way of reinforcing the command.

Stay

'Stay' training starts in a similar way to 'Wait', but instead of putting me in the sit position, tell me 'Down' so I can be comfortable. Start by standing beside me and say 'Down'. When I am lying down, take a step forwards with your right foot, holding your hand behind you with the palm facing me. I will probably get up and follow. Get me in the down position and try again. Eventually, you will be able to take a step forwards and then step back beside me without my moving. Praise me effusively when I do as you have asked. Always try to walk off with your right foot leading for the 'Stay' command, this is a visual clue for me. It will be surprisingly difficult for you to maintain this small detail, but it is important – it sends me a clear signal that I am doing a 'Stay' exercise.

As with teaching the 'Wait' command, extend the 'Stay' distance a little at a time. Keep repeating the word 'Stay' slowly, clearly and firmly. Turn and face me before you return to me. As I get even better at obeying you, when you have gone as far away from me as you wish, turn, face me and wait for five seconds before returning; continue to extend the time you wait at a distance: ten seconds, 20 seconds, 30 seconds, and so on.

In time, you will be able to leave me, return to me and walk around my rear, with me remaining in the downward position. I will be watching you closely the whole time. Always praise me calmly and quietly while I am still in the down position. Then release me with the 'Off you go' command.

Heel

Can I be blunt here? You move very slowly! Frankly, it tries my patience. I don't know why you can't move as quickly as I can, but it really is a source of intense frustration for me. You plod along like a tortoise, while I trot beside you with my dancing feet, tugging because I am desperate to move faster.

So, although I may not be the biggest or the heaviest dog, I will still try to drag you along in my wake when we go out on a walk because I want to hurry you along. There are so many things to see and smell.

Decide which side you want me to heel to and stick to it. In competitive obedience training I should be on your left, and because I respond to visual clues, you should always lead off with

your left foot first to reinforce the message that we are walking to heel. Remember, you lead with your right foot when we are doing a 'Stay' exercise. From the start, these consistent visual clues help me to understand and differentiate between what you want me to do. If you don't intend to show me competitively, choose whichever side suits you best; left-handed people may naturally prefer to have their whippet heel to their right-hand side (if this suits you better, just remember to consistently lead off with the opposite foot when you are teaching me the 'Stay' exercise).

If you are heeling to your left, hold the loop of the lead in your right hand and use your left hand to keep my head level with your legs. You are trying to keep my nose to the side of your leg. This may be too much of a challenge for me to begin with, but with lovely smelling treats in your hand, I should remain happily by your side.

Put high-status treats in your left pocket, then reach in with your left hand, get hold of a few treats and grasp them in your fist. Let your

hand hang by your side so that I can smell the treats, say 'Heel'. I will nose your hand in an effort to get at the treat. At very regular intervals give me a treat to keep me encouraged. Keep repeating the word 'Heel' over and over again while I am following your instruction.

Getting me to walk to heel will always be much easier on the way home as I will have had a good run around.

You can also train me to 'Heel' in the garden off lead, but always have those treats ready. We whippets really need a lot of incentive to learn to walk to heel, as it requires moving at a slower speed than we like.

If I am being resistant to walking to heel, another technique you can employ to encourage me to walk to heel is to keep changing direction without warning. This will throw me as I am expecting you to keep going forwards. Every time I start pulling, change direction again. It doesn't make for the most productive walk in terms of distance (and you might feel a little silly when other humans see you), but it will reinforce the notion that although you

are slower than me, I cannot always rely on you to plod along behind me. You are taking charge of our direction of travel. You are my pack leader and I will follow your lead.

I am a ball of energy, so you may find that even the most patient heel training is frustratingly slow to reap rewards. In this case, you might want to consider purchasing a Halti training collar.

A Halti has linked sections that run around the back of my head as well as loosely around my muzzle. I can still drink and pant with a Halti collar on. Instead of the lead attaching to the collar on my neck, it is attached to a loop under my muzzle. You are guiding me by my nose instead of by my powerful neck and it is very hard for me to pull.

Please get me used to the Halti before you try to take me out with it on. Put it on me, give me high-status treats, then take it off. Keep doing this. I will probably try to pull it off with my paw or by rubbing along the ground. Don't let me keep doing this. Take it off, then put it on again a few minutes later, give me a treat, take it off and repeat.

If you hold the tip of your nose with your fingers and pull it sideways you will see that your head automatically follows with no resistance. The Halti works on this principle. When I have worn a Halti consistently for a while, you will discover that I automatically walk to heel without pulling.

If you have just the one whippet, you can work on my walking to heel quite efficiently, but if you have two, you may find that Haltis are the perfect solution to your problem.

Leave

This command is designed to make me give up something without a fuss. It can be a life-saver (quite literally) if I have made off with something dangerous, such as a bar of chocolate accidentally left within my reach, a blister pack of painkillers I've taken from your handbag, or a cooked bone stolen from the bin as you clear up after lunch.

It can also have practical day-to-day advantages; while we are not natural retrievers, some whippets are very ball-focused and this can be a handy way of wearing us out quickly if you are short of time. However, it won't work as a strategy if you throw the ball once and I flatly refuse to give it up. Let's face it, if I run off with a ball, you aren't going to be able to catch me, though watching you try is quite entertaining.

Start training me young by gently trying to remove a toy from my mouth. Say 'Leave' in a firm but kind voice. If I hang on to the toy don't pull – tug is a fun game in itself. Just produce another toy and make it seem more exciting than the one I am clutching in my jaw. Say 'Leave' again and offer me the new toy. If I drop the old toy, make a fuss of me and give me the new toy. Reinforce this message over, and over, and over again.

The real secret to dog training is to understand that it is not something you ever, ever, ever stop doing. You can train me to sit and lie down on command, to wait and to stay exactly as instructed, but the one thing you can guarantee is that if you don't keep up the training, I won't carry on behaving beautifully indefinitely. More than anything else, with a whippet keep working on recall – every day, every single day!

Älli

Owned by Nea | Lives in Hämeenlinna, Finland | @vintintahtiin

Älli has plenty of energy and loves to run.
Together we do agility, racing, obedience and
tracking. He is quite vocal and 'talks' a lot. At
home he is most likely in the garden playing with
his ball or taking a nap.

Diet

hile whippets are natural thieves, very happy to steal sandwiches from a picnic, crisps or biscuits left on a table within reach, or the cold dregs from your tea or coffee cup, we tend not to be greedy. We can be faddy eaters, but don't assume this will be the case and indulge us – of course we will happily be fed sausages or ham from your hand when we have turned our nose up at the kibble complete diet you offered us for breakfast. We are very good at trying it on, and when we gaze at you with our hypnotic dark eyes it is hard to resist our pleas for treats.

Never leave a plate of food unattended within our reach. We may appear to be fast asleep, but the moment you leave the room, we will help ourselves to your dinner.

We are also adept at emotional blackmail. When you are dining, we will place our head lovingly in your lap and gaze up at you. Watch closely, and you will see that our eyes are actually following the course of your fork from plate to mouth, thus revealing our true intentions. We will work out who is the weakest link – the diner most likely to feed us titbits from their plate – and pile on the emotional pressure. If you don't want to encourage this behaviour, be firm from the start and don't feed me from your plate. You can still give me some leftovers, but put them into my bowl when you have finished eating. Don't hand-feed me from the table.

Being the food provider puts you in a position of power. The more you feed me treats from the table, the more my status is elevated and the less likely I am to pay attention to you, and this certainly includes my responding to a summons from you when we are out on a walk.

As a puppy, it is fine to feed me from bowls on the ground, but as I grow and my limbs lengthen, eating this way is uncomfortable. I will be very grateful if you buy me a stand to hold my food bowls at a more appropriate height. These can be adjusted so you can raise them as I get taller, always keeping my food and water at the perfect height for me.

Please don't feed me straight after a walk if I have been running free. Let me rest for half an hour before feeding. This is important; I can develop a twisted stomach or bloat, which is very dangerous. If you always leave an interval after exercise before feeding me, this problem shouldn't occur.

Weight

Whippets are not supposed to carry much fat (remember we are athletes even though we like to spend a huge amount of time sleeping). However, we should not be too thin either. If a whippet is the correct weight, you should be able to see and feel two to five bones of the spine and feel the undulation of the ribs beneath a layer of muscle. If we are having too much food and insufficient exercise, we will start to thicken around the waist, and you won't be able to feel our ribs or spine. I also won't be inclined to run as fast or as far, so will burn off fewer calories.

If this happens, it is time to put me on a diet. A high-fibre, low-fat complete food diet with fewer calories per pound can be utilized. I won't feel cheated if you feed me this, or you can just cut back on portions of my regular food. As with humans, carrying extra weight can lead to other health problems, including diabetes.

All dogs are omnivores, eating both plant and animal matter to survive. However, we cannot eat everything.

DO NOT give your whippet any of these foods:

- **Alcohol** isn't much good for humans and it's not good for whippets either. As well as all the obvious symptoms of alcohol poisoning - sickness and diarrhoea - it can also damage my central nervous system.

- **Avocado** contains persin, a fungicidal toxin that is harmless to humans, but which can cause vomiting and diarrhoea in dogs. It is present in the seed, the fruit, the skin and the leaves.

- **Caffeine** is not good for dogs. If we consume too much, it can have a similar effect to chocolate. Don't give us coffee or tea.

- **Chocolate** contains a compound called theobromine; it is fine for humans who can process it, but it can kill all dogs, even in small amounts. If your whippet has eaten chocolate, call the vet straight away and ask advice. Note how much chocolate has been consumed and whether it is dark or milk chocolate, as your vet will want to know; dark chocolate contains more theobromine. Depending on how much chocolate has been consumed, the vet may want to make your whippet vomit, and they may administer charcoal to absorb the poison.

- **Cooked bones** are highly dangerous. They can splinter and damage your whippet's internal organs, often causing perforation of the gut. Raw bones are safe, but only give your whippet a large raw bone, as small raw bones can cause choking and it's not worth the risk.

- **Corn-on-the-cob** is not poisonous to dogs, but it can

cause a blockage in our intestines and be potentially fatal.

- **Grapes, sultanas and raisins** can cause liver damage and kidney failure in some dogs. It is impossible to predict whether or not your whippet might be affected, so do not give us grapes, sultanas or raisins, and please think twice before you offer me a morsel of carrot cake or fruit cake!

- **Macadamia nuts** are toxic to dogs and can cause severe pain, muscle tremors and limb paralysis.

- **Onions, garlic and chives,** indeed anything from the onion family, are toxic to dogs and can cause serious gastrointestinal irritation and red blood cell damage.

- **Xylitol** is an artificial sweetener used in many low-fat and diet products, which is highly toxic to all dogs, including whippets.

It can induce hypoglycaemia, or low blood sugar, and is linked to liver failure and blood clotting disorders.

Nutrition

There is a huge variety of commercial dog food on the market and, as with human food, there is an increasingly sophisticated selection of products on offer. Wheat intolerance, gluten intolerance, hypoallergenic, vegan, sensitive tummies – all are catered for. You can feed your whippet a purely dry diet, a mix of wet and dry, cook your own meals as you might for a baby, have freshly cooked frozen meals delivered to your door or follow the unfortunately named BARF (Biologically Appropriate Raw Food) diet.

If you study the labels, you will find it hard to make direct comparisons of the nutrient content between different forms of dog food. Protein and fat are important components, as are a good balance of vitamins and minerals. Whippets need different quantities of nutrients at different stages of their lives; puppies have a much higher protein diet and the requirements of senior dogs (seven years and above) are different again to that of a lively adult whippet.

High-quality foods generally contain less in the way of fillers and more nutritional ingredients; cheaper foods will use more fillers to satisfy appetite.

Most adult dog foods contain around 20–30 per cent protein (5–8 per cent in wet foods) and 9–14 per cent fat (2–4 per cent in wet foods). Dietary fibre (vegetable matter) maintains intestinal health, helps to treat both constipation and diarrhoea and has a probiotic function. Ash is a measure of the mineral content of food and includes calcium, copper, iron, magnesium, manganese, phosphorus, potassium, selenium and zinc. There are 13 vitamins that are important for health: vitamin A, vitamin C, vitamin D, vitamin E, vitamin K and eight B vitamins.

Protein usually comes in the form of meat and fish, but vegetables can also supply proteins, and these protein sources are cheaper. Protein from non-meat sources, such as soya, maize and potato, are harder for a dog to digest and in some instances can cause dietary intolerance. Raw meat BARF diets have a much higher protein content and, as the meat is uncooked, it retains its nutrients. The nature of the protein content in dog food can vary from pure meat, to rendered meat meal, bone or animal derivatives.

Fats and oils are important for a whippets' skin and fur, and are also a good source of energy. Some essential fatty acids, such as omega-3, which are also important for health, are often added to commercial dog food.

Fillers make up the remaining percentage of dog food. This is likely to include whole grains, such as wheat, barley, corn, rice, oats, rye and sorghum, many of which also include important nutrients. They may also include peas, potatoes, sweet potatoes, quinoa and lentils, which are higher in calories.

As with all food purchases, you get what you pay for in theory, but your whippet may well be perfectly happy and thrive with a competitively priced dog food. If you are concerned

Marley & Bo

Owned by Ava and Ronan | Live in Dublin, Ireland | @itsmarleyandbo

Marley and Bo love hiking, city strolls, train
journeys, and beach zoomies. When they are not
busy exploring Ireland, you'll find them snoozing
on the sofa, barking at the birds, or getting up to
mischief in the garden.

about quality, don't rely on the front of the packaging for information: look at the ingredients listed on the back. If your whippet is thriving, everything is fine, but if they start to get tummy upsets or skin conditions, you may have to pay more careful attention to their diet. Always be guided by your vet. All dogs, including whippets, are less likely to develop food allergies than humans – they have robust digestive systems. Allergies to surroundings are more common irritants. Seek professional advice if we are getting skin disorders or runny poo on a regular basis – don't assume we have a food allergy.

Complete food, a specially formulated diet in the form of kibble, is perhaps the simplest way to ensure that your whippet gets a nutritionally balanced diet. If it is kept in an air-tight container it has a good shelf life.

Wet food, in the form of tins or pouches, is usually served with biscuits or kibble to ensure all the nutritional requirements are met.

The BARF diet imitates the diet a dog would have in the wild and is high in protein. It can be delivered frozen, and portions can be defrosted as required. Some whippets do very well on this diet, while others curl their lips at the notion of an uncooked dinner. If you choose to feed me the BARF diet, please follow all the usual hygiene precautions in handling raw meat, disinfecting all surfaces that have been in contact with raw meat and washing your hands.

In many countries around the world, you can also buy specially prepared, nutritionally appropriate, cooked meals online, which are then delivered frozen to your door. This is a premium product. I will love it, but it doesn't come cheap.

Water

Please make sure I always have water available and wash my water bowl daily. It isn't good for me to drink stale and dirty water – even though I may drink out of a puddle after I have been running flat out on a walk. Please keep some water in the car for me as well, along with a travelling water bowl, so that you can always offer me a drink. I will often need a drink at the end of a walk.

If you keep me well-fed and exercised, I will retain my beautiful physique. Get used to comments though: despite the fact that I can eat like a horse, you will constantly be advised by people who know no better that I could use some feeding up. Ignore them!

First Aid and Health

If you feed me right and give me plenty of exercise, I will stay healthy. Whippets are fortunate – the evolution of our breed has not led to the development of any significant health problems, unlike some of my purebred canine friends. I may get a little stiff in old age, but who doesn't?

Whippets do tend to be drama queens; the slightest knock will have us running back to you a whimpering, quivering wreck. It helps us if you give our hurt paw a rub for a minute or two. After some attention we will probably return happily to dashing around with our chums.

I am a speed freak and all that high-octane running means that, on occasion, I can come a cropper and, as with all accidents of this sort, the damage can be dramatic. It doesn't help that as I have such a short, fine coat, I bruise like a peach. A bramble will just get caught up in the coat of a long-haired dog, but it can rip my thin skin very easily. If I tear my ear while running, I will rapidly be covered head to toe in splashes of bright red blood – it looks worse than it is, but will certainly throw you into a panic when you first catch sight of me.

I can usually avoid sharp stones in my path when I am trotting along

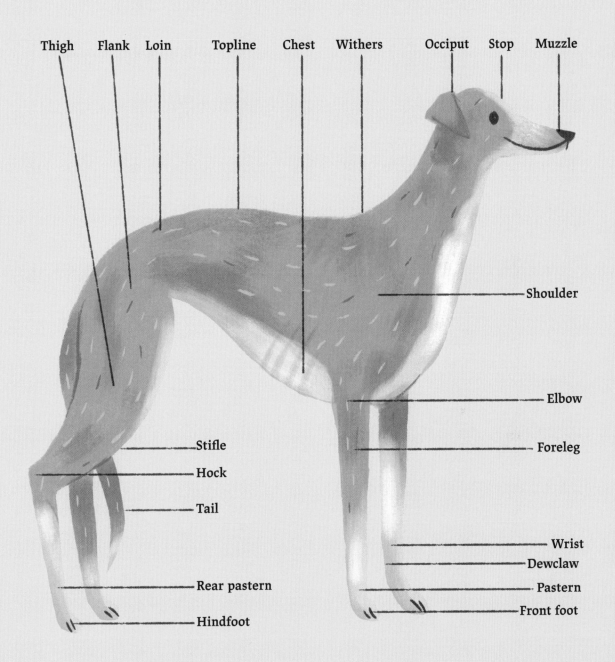

Thigh Flank Loin Topline Chest Withers Occiput Stop Muzzle

Shoulder

Elbow

Foreleg

Stifle

Hock

Tail

Wrist

Dewclaw

Rear pastern

Pastern

Hindfoot

Front foot

First-Aid Kit

Your canine first-aid kit should include:

- Antiseptic wipes
- Pressurized saline wound wash
- Antiseptic cream suitable for dogs
- Sterile gauze dressings
- Self-adhesive bandages
- A dog boot, in case of cut or injured paws.

beside you, but I won't if I'm running at full stretch. I am very proud of my ability to run at a record-breaking pace but, inevitably, I sometimes fail to slam on the brakes in time and collide with trees, hedges, low branches, noticeboards – you name it, I'll crash into it.

The net result is that if you are lucky enough to welcome a whippet into your home, at some point you will have to rush us to the vet with a cut something or other. So please, please, please get pet insurance in place right from the start, well before any accident occurs.

Pills and Medicine

Please never give me any form of human medicine, unless my vet specifically suggests it and advises the dosage.

Liquid medication is fairly easy to administer if you have a little doggy medicine syringe – nine times out of ten this comes with the medicine. The dose will be specified and marked on the syringe. Fill up the syringe to the required mark, then pop it into the side of my mouth, pointing the syringe towards my throat and squeeze quickly. This is usually a straightforward operation.

Pills can be more of a challenge. You can try holding my body gently between your legs, get the pill in one hand and with the other lift my head upwards and open my mouth. You want to drop the pill towards the back of my throat. Hold my jaws closed and stroke my throat to encourage me to swallow.

This may sound simple, but I am a master pill-spitter-outer. The vet may

tell you that the pills have a dog-friendly flavour, but we whippets are not easily fooled. If I generally have dry food, you can try popping the pill into some wet food and giving me that to eat, but be warned, I may find the pill and steer clear of it. And even if it works the first time, it may not after that. We are suspicious by nature and won't eat anything we don't like.

Alternatively, utilize something slightly moist, such as cream cheese or pâté to, quite literally, sweeten the pill. Pop the pill inside a little ball of something delicious, act like you are giving me a great treat, get me to sit and offer the camouflaged pill – the chances are I will wolf it down. Human foods are not good for us, but in extremis, small amounts can be utilized to fool us. Honestly, we are worse than small children when it comes to taking medicine.

Cuts

As mentioned earlier, the first time I injure myself it may look worse than it is, so try not to panic. If I have been running, my heart will be beating hard and fast, and I will be pumping blood out of my cut with some velocity. The first thing to do is to get me to sit down to slow my heartbeat. This will allow you to assess the severity of the injury. Apply gentle pressure to the cut. My skin is stretched quite tightly across my aerodynamic body, so cuts can gape. If this is the case, the cut is unlikely to heal without a stitch.

If you are unsure, please contact my vet straight away for advice, lift me in and out of the car and don't let me do anything active until I have been checked out. If stitches are required, the sooner it is done the better, although I will be ungrateful and won't thank you. The vet will have to anaesthetize me and may need to keep me in overnight. I will be very wobbly after an anaesthetic, and I may well have to be carried into the house. I won't know what to do with myself and will probably just stand looking dazed. Pick me up, put me on my bed or the sofa close to you, and cover me up with a blanket. I will sleep.

I will also need the 'cone of shame' (buster collar) because I will not leave any stitches or dressing alone. I must not be allowed to worry at my stitches, although I won't understand why you won't let me. This specially designed, elongated collar prevents me from doing any damage to myself, despite my best efforts, and I will try my best to get the collar off. You will have to leave it on at night, or you will wake to find I have removed the dressing and all of my stitches and this will mean another trip to the vet, which is costly for you and traumatic for me. Be firm.

The collar can come off on walks and for meals – I will be able to access my water bowl with it on no matter what I would have you believe.

If my foot has been injured, you may have to cover it with some kind of plastic shoe so that the dressing doesn't get wet; even in the summer the grass will be covered with dew in the morning.

I will need to be on lead walks for a minimum of ten days – the vet will guide you. The vet will want to give me regular check-ups to ensure that everything is healing as it should, and any dressings will need to be regularly changed. Even if I seem to be healing nicely, don't let me off the lead until the vet gives me the all-clear. I can rip stiches open if I am allowed to run free.

Heat Exhaustion

All dog owners should be aware that you must not leave us in cars in full sun or even in the shade when it is hot. Although it may not feel that warm, a car can heat up very quickly. Conservatories and caravans can also be dangerous. When it is 22°C (72°F) outside, the interior temperature of a car can quickly rise to 47°C (117°F).

To keep us safe, it is best not to leave us in the car alone at all. With the best intentions in the world, even five minutes can be too long, because as you know shops can have queues, or you can bump into someone you know, and before you know it half an hour has passed, and I am dying due to the heat.

By the same token, you should be careful when you travel with me on long journeys. Give me frequent breaks, the chance to stretch my legs, relieve myself, have a drink and relax in the shade.

We can also get heat exhaustion on a summer walk if you allow us to run too much. If we suddenly head into the sea, or a river and lower our bodies into the water to cool down, it is a sign that we have been overdoing it. Ball fanatics won't stop chasing after a ball you are throwing for them because they are getting too hot. If there is no water nearby, we will have no way of cooling down. If I seem disorientated, confused or start swaying, I have become dangerously overheated.

The first thing to do is to cool me down. Spraying me with a hose will be too much of a shock to my system. Instead, wet a large towel with cold water and place it over me. Gently sprinkle cold water over the towel every few minutes to keep it cool – a watering can with a sprinkler head will do the job perfectly. Overheating to this extent can cause long-term damage and I should be checked out by the vet. It can take me a few days to recover from heat exhaustion.

This is a shocking experience for me and for you, so please don't let me run around like a mad thing on a hot day.

Diarrhoea

If I have diarrhoea, the chances are that either you have made a dramatic alteration to my diet, which may not suit me, or, and this is the more likely of the two, that I have scavenged something to eat that has not agreed with me. As already mentioned in Chapter 3, although whippets are not greedy, we are great thieves and like nothing more than chomping on something illicit we find on a walk.

The first course of action is to withhold food for a day, but please make sure I have water on hand, as diarrhoea can lead to dehydration. After 24 hours, feed me something bland: cooked chicken with boiled rice is ideal. I will enjoy this! Just give me a small portion and allow me plenty of time to digest it before giving me a little bit more. This will usually sort everything out and I can return to normal feeding. However, if things don't improve, please take me to the vet.

If you see blood in my faeces, or if I am vomiting as well, contact the vet straight away.

Silva

Owned by Drifa | Lives in Iceland | @whippet_silva

Silva is calm, sweet, and very smart. She loves being in the beautiful Icelandic outdoors. Her favourite toys are balls on strings that she can chase and shake. She is so easy to manage and extremely patient.

Vomiting

I will vomit sometimes – all dogs do, even the elegant whippet. Sometimes this may be because I have gobbled my food down too quickly. If this happens you will probably be horrified to see me happily tucking in to the whole regurgitated mess all over again. Greedy puppies are especially prone to this, so if it happens regularly, feed me the same amount but split it into smaller portions more times a day. Don't let me run around straight after eating.

I quite like to eat grass, but I may vomit after eating it. This is nothing to worry about.

If I vomit repeatedly, I may have eaten something unpleasant. Follow the same principle of withholding food for 24 hours, and then feeding me a bland diet.

If I am vomiting frequently, or if you notice something resembling blood or faecal matter – and that smells really foul – take me straight to the vet.

Coughing

A very occasional cough is nothing to worry about, but a regular cough should be checked out by my vet.

Kennel cough is an airborne disease, usually a virus, that easily spreads between dogs. I can be inoculated annually against kennel cough and the vaccination will lower my chances of catching it and reduce my symptoms if I do. Most boarding kennels insist that I am inoculated against kennel cough before a stay. If I am not vaccinated, I can pick up kennel cough from infected dogs. Most dogs with kennel cough aren't too poorly, but some of us can be badly affected and may need anti-inflammatories to bring down our temperature and reduce inflammation in our airways.

You will need to keep me away from other dogs for 2–3 weeks after my symptoms have disappeared. Don't let me race around if I have kennel cough, as this can make symptoms worse. Instead, give me gentle exercise on a lead.

A cough can also be indicative of heart disease, especially if it happens after exercise or in the evening. Get me checked out by a vet who will listen to my heart to make sure that this isn't the cause of the coughing.

Ears

I have beautiful ears, described by experts as 'rose-shaped'. They generally hang forwards, but when I am hot, I will fold them back to allow air to circulate. If I am interested in something on a walk, I may prick my ears upright. As my ears are so mobile, and my fur short, they tend to be healthy with no sign of inflammation or discharge.

If I start scratching my ear or shaking my head, have a look inside: there may be a grass seed, a burr or some other foreign body that is causing discomfort. If you can see something obvious, remove it gently – damp cotton wool is good for this. Don't probe into the ear or use ear buds. If the foreign body doesn't lift out easily, I will need a trip to the vet.

If you can see a dark discharge in the ear that looks like coffee grounds, I may have ear mites. Once again, a trip to the vet is in order. Over-the-counter products are not recommended – please consult an expert. (See page 88 for more information on ear mites).

Skin Irritation

Skin allergies can have a number of trigger factors: oversensitivity can be caused by fleas (see pages 80–83 for more on fleas), pollen, grass, moulds, house dust mites and some foods. The skin becomes itchy, red and can be hot to the touch. Bald patches and skin infections can develop. Please make an appointment for me to see the vet if you are concerned; skin problems tend to get worse if they are left untreated and the vet will help you to determine what my trigger factors might be.

Whippets are not especially prone to skin problems, however a friend of mine used to develop sore feet every September and the problem would clear up by the end of October. It seemed to be an allergy to wet grass that occurred only at this time of year. His poor feet puffed up and turned red and sore, and he would lick them furiously, which only made matters worse. He would walk stiffly on his swollen feet and ankles, and would have to be lead walked on pavements until November, when the

problem magically disappeared for another year.

Bites

If you own a dog, any dog, the chances are that at some point they will become involved in some nose-to-nose power posturing with another dog. Whippets, being on the small side, are not natural guard dogs. We don't look for trouble and because of our running skills we avoid confrontation by taking off, secure in the knowledge that we won't be caught. Trapped on the lead it might be another story; we can be more vocal, full of sound and fury, signifying nothing, and you might see our hackles rising, just to be on the safe side.

The fact is that whippets in a fight tend to come off worse – it's our thin skin again. One small nip will provoke terrible crying and swift submission, and a large bite can cause serious injury. Once again, a trip to the vet may be required to ensure I don't need stitches and to administer antibiotics, as dog bites generally lead to infection.

Wasps and Bees

Whippets will also suffer irritation if they are stung by wasps or bees. First, check to make sure that the sting itself is not stuck in our skin. If it is, remove it carefully, scraping it out rather than pulling it as this can release more venom. Bathe the area with cool water to help reduce the swelling. Most dogs suffer minor pain and irritation, but if the area is swelling rapidly or if the dog is having difficulty breathing or vomiting, take it straight to the emergency vet.

Snake Bites

Snake bites can be fatal. In the UK it is only the adder that can cause whippets serious harm, but in countries such as America and Australia, there are far more venomous snakes that can strike. If you see your whippet worrying something in the grass, call them to you immediately.

The majority of snake bites occur during the spring and summer months. If you think your whippet has been bitten, keep them quiet and calm and take them to the vet as a matter of urgency. If you see the snake attack, make a note of its markings as this will help the vet administer the correct anti-venom. You can tie a constricting band above the bite to slow the spread of the venom. This should be snug but not too tight.

Snake-Bite Symptoms

If you are worried that your dog may have been bitten by a poisonous snake, symptoms to look out for include:

- A small wound with fang marks
- Swelling of the affected area
- Collapse (though they can recover temporarily)
- Sudden weakness
- Vomiting
- Hypersalivation
- Dilated pupils
- Twitching of the muscles.

Fireworks

Humans seem to like fireworks, but we whippets don't share your enthusiasm. Prevention is the best cure: don't take me to a firework display and don't let me be anywhere near fireworks going off. If I wasn't frightened by fireworks before, I will become hypersensitive to them if I am near some going off.

The best thing you can do is to avoid creating a phobia in the first place. If you know there are going to be fireworks in the vicinity of your home, keep me indoors. Take me for a good walk before it gets dark, so that I won't need toilet breaks during the evening. Turn up the volume on the television or the radio to drown out the noise, and don't leave me at home alone. Stay calm and ignore any bangs to give me the message that this is not something I need to worry about. If there are a lot of bright flashes you can cover me up with a blanket, so I don't notice them so much.

If your whippet does become sensitized, this can become a problem. Whippets have been known to take off in blind terror at the first bang of a firework. The noise is terrible to our sensitive ears and our first response is flight. When we stop running and hiding, we will then be panic-stricken because we have lost you and are now alone, far from home, with no idea where we are.

If my phobia is severe, the vet can recommend some natural therapies and possibly pheromone treatments to make me feel more secure. Tranquillizers are a very last resort, but even these won't cure the terror, just make us very sleepy.

All dogs look sad when they are unwell, but the whippet face of woe is positively tragic; it's a performance worthy of an Oscar. We can – and will – put it on for the smallest knock, and we will wear it and keep you on your nursing toes, until the pain is gone. Then, as if by magic, when the vet gives us the all-clear, and you are allowed to let us off lead once again, we will run and run and run and run and our hearts will be full of joy!

Bolt & Dash

Owned by Sebastien and Sacha | Live in California | @whippetsunleased

An enthralling pair, Bolt and Dash spread joy
and garner attention wherever they go. They are
confident, compassionate, and always playful.

Grooming

Many whippet owners compare us to cats. We are self-cleaning and quite fastidious in our personal hygiene; we lick ourselves clean after we have been to the toilet. We carefully clean our feet and pads after every walk and will work to remove any splashes of mud on our coat. We are certainly not smelly dogs, although like all of our kind, our flatulence is silent but deadly.

We pick our way around puddles and mud on a walk and won't want to swim in the river or the sea. However, if we get hot on a walk during the summer, we may lower ourselves carefully into the water, keeping our head up and our tail high and dry, to cool ourselves down quickly.

The result of this is that we won't need bathing very often. This is good news because we really don't enjoy a shower or a bath – although it helps no end if the water is lovely and warm.

Bathing

If you need to bathe me, wet me thoroughly then apply a dog shampoo – a human shampoo can give me skin irritation – and give me a good rub all over to clean my fur. Rinse me gently, making sure you remove all traces of

the shampoo, as any residue will make me sore. Please avoid getting any water in my ears – it might trigger an ear infection. If possible, don't wet my face at all. It can be washed separately with a clean cloth dipped in warm water, then wrung out.

Once I am clean, have lots of warm towels to hand. Put one on the floor, place me on it and then put another towel on top of me. Rub me briskly. I will enjoy this. When you release me, I will run wildly all over the house in a state of high excitement and rub myself on your carpets and soft furnishings to dry myself off even more. If it's not cold, let me into the garden and I will race around until I feel like myself again.

If you ever use a hose on me, I will fight to escape the brutal assault of cold water. Some dogs don't mind a hose, but whippets hate them!

Grooming us will help us to keep ourselves clean, and if you use the right equipment, we will enjoy being groomed once a week. This is a good opportunity for you to give me the once-over and make sure I am healthy with no unexplained lumps and bumps.

I have short hair and am thin, so I don't enjoy being combed with a metal comb – it hurts me. Please use a soft brush instead, but be gentle. The aim is to dislodge any dust or dirt in my coat.

I will also enjoy being stroked with a grooming glove – this has rubber nodules all over it and it is like being given a gentle massage – I love it and it will pull off masses of loose hair. Start with my head and then move down my body. Do give my thighs a good rub – I adore this and will stand still for you.

If you want to go for a professional finish, show dogs are smoothed over with a chamois leather before an event, which enhances the shine of the coat. Show whippets are never washed immediately before an event as bathing is drying, so our coat loses its gloss for a few days.

Check-up

When you have groomed me, please give me a check over and make sure my eyes are bright. Clean away any debris in the corner of my eyes with some damp cotton wool. Take a peek into my ears: they should be clean and shouldn't need any attention, but if there is any debris, clean them gently with some damp cotton wool. Foreign bodies such as grass seeds can cause irritation, or you might spot ear mites, which look like coffee grounds in my ear canal. Mites will need to be treated by a vet. A word of caution: *don't* use cotton buds in my ears – I am designed differently from you.

Smile Please!

You can help to keep my teeth clean by giving me raw bones to chew, or you can buy specially designed chews that are supposed to help prevent the build-up of plaque and tartar. Feeding me dry food and hard dog biscuits is also helpful.

If I develop bad breath, this may indicate gum disease, and a serious build-up of tartar will require the vet to give my teeth a deep clean. This must be done under anaesthetic; it's an unnecessary expense for you and I certainly won't enjoy the experience. What's more, neglecting my teeth can lead to the development of other serious health problems.

You can also clean my teeth every couple of days. I know this sounds crazy! Use special dog-friendly toothpaste, which tastes of meat, so I don't mind the experience. Do not use human toothpaste on me – it can be harmful. To start with, rub the toothpaste over a couple of my teeth to get me used to the sensation, and gradually increase the amount of toothpaste and time spent on the task over a week or so. If I become used to you manipulating my lips you will be able to clean all the surfaces of my teeth, either using a small toothbrush or a specially designed finger brush that slips over your finger. Give me plenty of treats to reward me for standing still and cooperating.

Ask the vet to check my teeth occasionally, perhaps when I go in for my annual inoculation, just to make sure no problems are developing.

Pedicure

My nails grow like yours and shouldn't be allowed to get too long. Pavement walking helps to keep them in shape, but you will still need to trim them. Get someone who knows how to show you how to perform this task before trying it at home. If you are not confident, leave nail-trimming to the professionals.

My nails contain the quick – the vessel that brings blood to the nails. If you cut my nails too short you will cut this; it will be painful and I will bleed. It will also mean I won't want you to come anywhere near my nails again.

If you can hear my nails clicking when I walk across a hard floor, it is a sign that my nails are too long. Long, uncut nails can lead to lameness.

Little and often is the best policy for pedicures. If you trim my nails every two weeks, you will only need to take off a small piece of the nail. I will be suspicious of this process initially, but in time I will relax and behave while you give me my pedicure. You will become more confident in performing this procedure and will be able to cut a little closer to the quick.

I am naturally a clean and elegant hound and my grooming requirements are minimal; please keep up with my beauty regime as I like to look my best at all times.

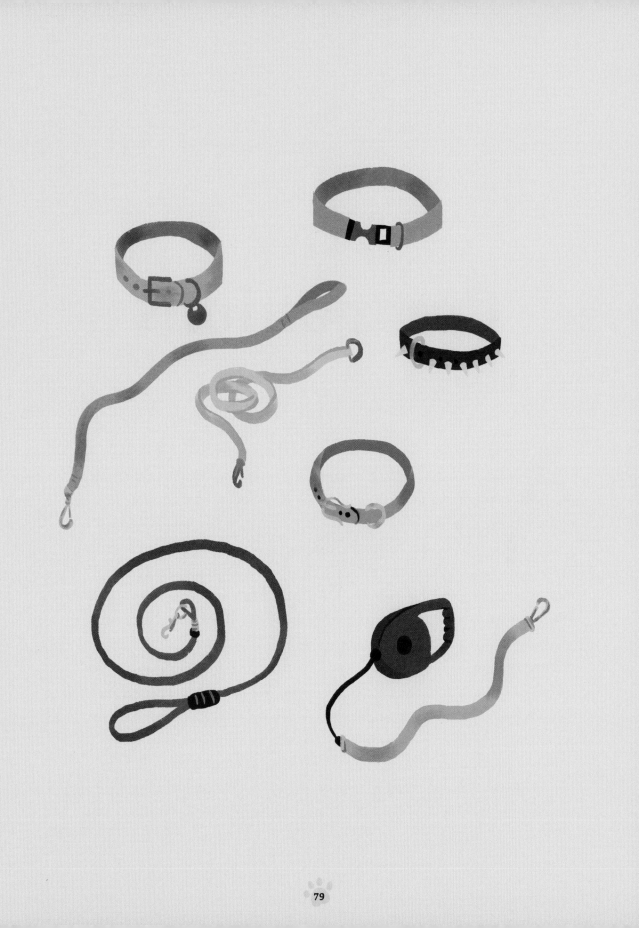

Tiny Companions

All animals accommodate a host of tiny friends and even I, the elegant whippet, am no exception!

Fleas

As sure as night follows day, I will get fleas. Fleas are everywhere; cats and humans shouldn't get too squeamish about them because you have your own cat fleas and human fleas too. I can pick them up from another dog, a cat, your home, your friend's home or from your clothes or your shoes.

These tiny parasites are superb jumpers, which is how they hop from their environment, to host, to home, to host and so on. Females must have a meal of blood before they lay their eggs and can lay up to 50 eggs per day. The eggs are like tiny grains of sand. They fall off me when they are laid, then hatch into larvae within 2–5 days. The larvae, which are around 0.5cm (¼ in) long, live in carpets, soft furnishings and cracks in the floorboards. They feed, and after around two weeks build a cocoon, from which they emerge as adult fleas when a food source is nearby. The entire life cycle takes around 3–4 weeks. Fleas can also pass on tapeworms to me (see page 86).

Fleas are particularly active when the weather is warmer, but they can still reproduce inside the home in winter. Moreover, fleas can lie dormant in a home for a long time when there is no food source, but the arrival of a pet stimulates them to hatch. If you are moving house, make sure my flea treatments are up to date.

Dog fleas prefer dogs, cat fleas prefer cats, but they will hop on any host in extremis, even you! If you are being bitten by fleas, it suggests that our home has a serious flea problem.

If I have fleas, bear in mind that only approximately 5 per cent of the flea population will be on me. The remaining 95 per cent will be in our home! Spot-on treatments, which are very effective, only kill the adult fleas, so if there is an infestation, it can take up to three months to eradicate the problem. The best solution is to consistently use appropriate preventative flea treatments from the moment I come into your life as a puppy.

Puppies require specific flea treatments suitable for their age and weight. The earliest this can be administered is usually at eight weeks. Some treatments are not suitable for young puppies, so you should always consult your vet for advice. Fleas can trouble puppies badly; they can have an adverse reaction to flea bites leading to allergic dermatitis, and in severe infestations a puppy can develop life-threatening anaemia.

How can you tell whether I have fleas? Scratching is a tell-tale sign, but you can see evidence of fleas too: part my coat at the back of my neck, near my ears or at the base of my tail and look for tiny black specks that resemble pepper. This is flea dirt, basically digested blood and very unsavoury. If you put this on a piece of paper and dampen it, it will turn red and this is proof I have fleas.

Chemical spot-on treatments, which are administered to the back of the neck and between the shoulder blades, are very effective. These will also kill all the flea eggs. Live fleas will be killed within 24 hours and some flea treatments also kill ticks.

Please remember to wash my pet bedding regularly, hoover floors thoroughly and don't forget the soft furnishings. Empty the contents of the dust bag after hoovering!

If you follow this regime, fleas should never become a problem. However, if you do let things slide and your house has a serious flea infestation – you will probably be being bitten too at this point – you will also need to use a chemical spray treatment on your house to help kill the pesky things.

If you want to use 'natural' herbal preparations, please check with your vet first. Ironically, the ingredients in some products are not safe for use around dogs or cats. Cat-flea treatments are not safe for use on dogs either and vice versa!

Ticks

Like fleas, ticks will climb onto me when I am out on a walk, then enjoy a drink of my blood. The tick will stay in place until it has had enough to drink when it will drop off. Quite apart from being unsightly, ticks can cause severe skin irritation and can also transmit Lyme disease or borreliosis, a nasty tick-transmitted bacterial infection that

Lyme Disease Symptoms

These might include:

- Fever
- Lethargy
- Limping
- Swollen lymph nodes (situated in the neck, chest, the tops of the front legs, groin and behind the knees of the rear legs).

occurs in Europe, North America and Asia, and which can affect humans as well as dogs.

Ticks are very common in areas where there is wildlife or livestock, and are most commonly seen in warmer weather. They start off very small but grow as they feed; you can see or feel them on me, and my short coat usually ensures they are spotted quite quickly.

Ticks resemble a skin tag and can be light in colour, grey or quite dark. The part you can see is the tick's large, flat body. Don't attempt to pull it straight off me; this can result in cross-

Lolly

Owned by Elisa and Sam | Lives in London | @lollythewhippet

A sweet, sensitive soul who has brought love
and joy to our lives. She's happiest when we're
exploring the countryside, spending time at the
beach or curling up for a snuggle on the sofa at
the end of a long day.

contamination as parts of the mouth can remain in situ.

Ticks are easily removed with a tick tool, which allows you to anchor the body of the tick, while you then twist the tool. This effectively unscrews the tick from its food source. Once you have removed the tick, squash it very hard between some paper and dispose of the body. It is best to purchase a tick tool when you get a puppy, so you always have it to hand when needed. You can buy a cheap tick tool from most pet shops.

If you are worried that I may have contracted Lyme disease from a tick, take me to the vet.

Worms

Dogs can and will pick up worms from numerous sources: soil, vegetation or faeces can be contaminated with worm eggs, and contaminated fleas can pass on tapeworms to your dog. Worms can be transmitted from dog to dog via their faeces and though it is unusual, they can also be passed on to you. This is another good reason for all dog owners to scoop the poop! Worms can cause diarrhoea and vomiting, weight loss, weakness, coughing and anaemia. Puppies with worms develop an abnormally swollen tummy. If you see me scooting - dragging my bottom along the floor - this is an indication that I may have worms, though I can do this for other reasons too, so get me checked out by the vet.

Intestinal Worms

- **Roundworms** are passed on to a puppy via its mother's milk and adult dogs can contract them from contaminated soil or meat. These look like spaghetti in your dog's poo, but spaghetti that wriggles around!

- **Hookworms and whipworms** live in my intestines, where they latch on with sharp teeth to suck my blood. Weight loss is a common symptom and I contract them via contaminated soil.

- **Tapeworms** are spread by infected fleas. They can also be spotted around my anus and look like grains of rice in my poo but are actually small segments of the tapeworm. I pick them up if I accidentally ingest an infected flea while grooming myself. As the flea is digested, the tapeworm egg is released and hatches, whereupon it latches onto my small intestine. Occasionally, an entire tapeworm can be passed or vomited up – not a pleasant experience for anyone, so keep on top of my flea control!

All dogs should be regularly wormed, and there are numerous deworming medications available. Puppies are at particular risk from worms but please seek advice from your vet before worming your puppy.

Lungworm

Lungworm (*Angiostrongylus vasorum*), is fairly common in some countries and it can kill. I can contract it if I consume its larvae, which are found in infected slugs, snails and frogs. Dogs can accidentally eat small slugs if they are on their toys or their fur. The lungworm moves through the dog's body and finally settles in the heart and blood vessels. We excrete the larvae in our poo. This infects more slugs and snails, which in turn can infect more dogs.

Take your dog to the vet to be checked out if they are displaying any of the symptoms listed below; the vet will need to prescribe a special course of medication to eliminate lungworm. In some areas, where lungworm is especially prevalent, it is advisable to give your dog preventative medication.

Lungworm Symptoms
These might include:
- Coughing
- Breathing problems
- Reluctance to exercise
- Abnormal blood clotting

Heartworm

Dirofilariasis is an infection caused by parasites of the genus *Dirofilaria* that is transmitted via the bite of an infected mosquito and affects dogs, cats and ferrets. It is found in large swathes of the USA and Canada but is rarely seen in the UK. There are 30 species of mosquito that transmit it. Heartworm kills dogs, but as it takes several years before symptoms appear, the disease is often well-advanced by the time clinical signs are visible. Blood tests can confirm a diagnosis and X-rays will show the extent of the damage. Medication is given via a series of injections. It is critical that dogs are kept quiet during treatment and for several months afterwards, which is not easy with a whippet. If you live in an area where heartworm can be contracted, preventive medication is recommended.

Heartworm Symptoms

These might include:

- Dry cough
- Shortness of breath
- Listlessness
- Loss of stamina

Mites and Mange

These two conditions are uncomfortable rather than life-threatening but can be costly for you and distressing for us, so as with many things, prevention and regular treatment are the rules here.

Mites

- **Ear mites** (*Otodectes cynotis*), are common in cats but can affect dogs too, so if your dog has ear mites always check their feline friends as well. The parasites live in the outer ear canal. Symptoms include ear scratching and shaking of the head. The ear will become red and inflamed and you may see a waxy brown discharge. Untreated ear mites can lead to other ear infections. The ear will need to be regularly cleaned and treated with medicated ear drops prescribed by the vet.

Regular flea treatment should act as a preventative.

- **Fur mites** (*Cheyletiella* spp.) cause cheyletiellosis, commonly dubbed 'walking dandruff'. These small white mites live on the surface of the skin and cause mild itchiness. One of the obvious signs of a fur mite infestation is a coat full of small flakes of skin or scurf.

- **Harvest mites** (*Trombicula* spp.), are small orange mites that can also affect cats and humans. They can easily be picked up in grassy areas or woodland in late summer and autumn. This mite causes intense itching and inflammation in the feet and lower legs, but it can also affect the armpits, the tummy, the genitals and very occasionally the ears. It can be seen with the naked eye. It is easily treated with an insecticide, and anti-inflammatories may be required to ease discomfort. Regular flea treatments should deal with this problem without it ever becoming an issue.

Mange

There are two types of skin mites that can cause mange: *Demodex canis* and *Sarcoptes scabiei*.

A dog with a good immune system should not fall prey to demodectic mange, but puppies can be at risk as they cannot stop the parasite and it is usually passed from mother to pup. The parasite lives within the hair follicles and causes the skin to become very itchy, which can lead to hair loss and the development of lesions. It spreads from the point of infection and across the whole body; the dog's skin appears to turn a blue-grey. This form of mange does not easily spread to other dogs or to humans and is treated with a topical preparation.

Scabies, however, is highly contagious. All dogs in the household will need to be treated with a medicated shampoo. This is a zoonotic disease, which means it can be passed on to humans. Foxes are a common source of contagion.

Fascinating Whippet Facts

- **The fastest** recorded sprint for a whippet is 10.8 seconds for a 200-yard (182.8m) dash. This makes an average speed of 38 ½ miles per hour (62 km/h).

- **Whippets have** what is known as a double suspension gait: when we run, our front legs extend in front of us and our rear legs extend out behind us; during full extension all four of our paws are off the ground.

- **Whippets shiver** easily because we don't have a lot of fat and our coats are short and thin, offering little protection against cold, wind or rain.

- **When whippets** are a healthy weight, we should have two to five visible vertebrae on our backs. If you can see more, your whippet is underweight; if you can see less, it is overweight.

- **Whippets need** special collars because of our long necks: wider collars reduce pressure on our throats.

- **Whippets don't** bark very much, though we will usually alert you to the arrival of the postman or the milkman!

- **Whippets have** a strong prey drive; we are always scanning the horizon for something we can chase.

- **Kuiper the science dog** is a whippet with 156,000 followers on Instagram. At the time of writing, he is the most popular whippet on social media. Take a peek at @spacewhippet.

- **Pluto, Lucien Freud's** whippet, was a regular sitter for this famous artist.

- **The American Kennel** Club formally recognized the whippet as a breed in 1888, four years after it was founded. The UK Kennel Club followed suit three years later, in 1891.

- **Toby the whippet** holds the Guinness World Record for the fastest time to pop 100 balloons, coming in at an impressive 36.56 seconds.

- **Whippets are** the fastest accelerating dogs in the world. Off the mark, a whippet leaves a greyhound behind, but the greyhound would catch up and overtake over a distance as their greater weight, muscle mass and larger heart give them the race advantage.

Seymour

Owned by Nadja | Lives in South London | @occamstores

Seymour is an introvert with extrovert
tendencies. He's shy at first but once you win him
over, he's the most loyal and excitable whippet.
Together we go on adventures in our little van,
exploring the UK for the best beaches to picnic
and play on.

Index

Further reading

Coile D Caroline, *Whippets*, Barron's Educational Series, 1998

Cunliffe Juliette, *Sight Hounds*, Swan Hill Press, 2006

Duffy R (Series Editor), *Whippets*, BX Plans Ltd, 2020

Fielding Jeff, *Whippet*, 2016

Fitch Daglish E, *Whippets*, W&G Foyle Ltd, 1964

Garfield Simon, *Dog's Best Friend*, W&N, 2021

McConkey Molly and Phillips-Griffiths Rebecca, *Whippet*, Pet Book Publishing, 2013

Walsh E.G. and Lowe Mary, *The English Whippet*, The Boydell Press, 1985

Walsh E.G., *Lurchers and Longdogs*, The Standfast Press, 1977

Acknowledgements

My first thanks must go to Jimmy the Lurcher, our first family dog, who turned this cat-loving, dog-hating mother-of-two into an ardent dog-worshipper. Jimmy was a living, breathing incarnation of a badly behaved dog and together we discovered how dog training can transform your life. Dog behaviourist Charles Scott was entirely responsible for his gradual transformation to perfectly behaved pooch.

So charmed was I by dog ownership, that Rosie the whippety lurcher joined the pack. Rosie was my girl from the first. A determined hunter, she could keep going like a Duracell bunny long after Jimmy, a sprinter, had tired. She loved nothing better than to lie on the sofa with her head in my lap. RIP Rosie and Jim.

Betsey Trotwood, a beautiful whippet, has shared my life for the last five years. She patiently taught me how to live with whippets. She is a pampered princess who feels the cold terribly and whose arrival brought joy into my life. Betsey has been joined by Billy Bremner, a tough four-year-old northern whippet, who has no truck with coats and who struggles to keep up with his idol Betsey, who can run like the wind. He is a complete softie who loves his sleep. This naughty pair rule my life and delight me daily.

I must thank my husband, Eric, without whose patient nagging I would never have discovered that dog-owning was a good thing. For this and all kinds of other things, I owe him a huge debt of gratitude. Our children, Florence and Teddy, have patiently endured their parents' dog worshipping tendencies and embraced the delights of dog walking in the rain.

Florence must also be thanked for taking the time to proofread the first draft of this book. Despite being very busy and important, she patiently corrects my punctuation and makes all kinds of helpful suggestions.

At Batsford I must, as always, thank Polly Powell for her faith in me. Lilly Phelan has been the kindest and gentlest of editors and a delight to work with, and Gemma Doyle must be thanked for her superb design.